HOW THE FUTURE BEGAN

MACHINES

HOW THE FUTURE BEGAN

MACHINES

CLIVE GIFFORD

KING*f*ISHER

KING*f*ISHER

Kingfisher Publications Plc
New Penderel House,
283–288 High Holborn,
London WC1V 7HZ

Author
Clive Gifford

Senior Editor
Clive Wilson

Senior Designer
Mike Buckley

DTP Co-ordinator
Nicky Studdart

Senior Production Controller
Caroline Jackson

Picture Research Manager
Jane Lambert

Picture Researcher
Juliet Duff

Indexer
Sue Lightfoot

First published by Kingfisher Publications Plc 1999
1 3 5 7 9 10 8 6 4 2

1TR/0799/TWP/RNB(RNB)/135NYMA

Copyright © Kingfisher Publications Plc 1999

A CIP catalogue record for this book is available from
the British Library.

ISBN 0 7534 0318 8

Printed in Singapore

CONTENTS

It is almost impossible to imagine a world without machines. Cars, aircraft, computers, factories and communication networks have transformed almost every aspect of our lives. Machines have helped us to move faster, work more efficiently, and given us more free time. They have transported us underwater and into space – journeys we could once have only dreamed of. Where machines will take us in the future is limited only by our imagination.

Ever since our ancestors first used stone tools, humans have been using machines. For most of history, machines were simple devices that channelled mechanical force supplied by human or animal muscles. Then, in the 1700s, the invention of the steam engine kickstarted the Industrial Revolution and propelled us into a new era, one dominated by increasingly sophisticated and powerful machines.

During the 21st century, advances in computer technology will make machines smarter and even more powerful. Many machines will function with the minimum of human intervention. Robot carers will look after the sick, remote vehicles will explore hazardous places and tiny robots will perform delicate surgery deep inside the body. And in the more distant future, machines may even enable the human race to colonize other planets.

Some of the predictions made in this book may not happen, while other unexpected developments may occur. But one thing is for certain – machines will continue to flourish and shape our future.

1970s Use of composite materials e.g. in fighter aircraft

1960s Early development of smart materials

1961 First industrial robot, built by Unimation

1908 First mass production assembly line

1903 Development of stainless steel

1767 Spinning jenny first machine to spin many threads at a time

1728 Falcon's loom uses punch card system

MACHINES IN INDUSTRY

People have been using machines ever since the first prehistoric human scraped an animal hide with a sharpened flint edge, or moved a large rock with a stick as a lever. Machines have developed in complexity as we have learned how to use and control aspects of the world around us – from making and shaping materials such as metals to manipulating forces such as electricity and air pressure.

The 20th century saw a revolution in the way many people work. Much of that is down to machines, from the rise of mass production in factories with its dependence on machines and automation, to the invention of the computer which has transformed millions of jobs. In the 21st century, humans will supervise robots and automated machine workers, often at long distance, as the remote, automated factory becomes a reality. With giant leaps in nanotechnology and micro-engineering, communications technology and new materials, the products of the future may not only be very different from today's but may also be manufactured in completely new ways.

Fully dextrous multi-
purpose robot in use
2008

Smart metal alloys used
for domestic objects
2006

First molecular
machines designed
1990s

First use of robots in
nuclear power plants
1988

VR and automation
allow customization via
remote factories
2015

Nano-robots used in
surgery
2060

ROBOTS AT WORK

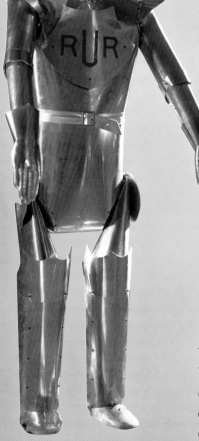

Although there are currently thousands of robots at work all over the world, robotics – the study, design and improvement of robots – is still in its infancy. Even so, many robots perform tasks that are impossible for humans and do some jobs more quickly and accurately than us. However, developments in robotics are expected to take place, creating far more flexible, versatile, affordable machines that will be able to work with little or no human intervention. Whatever the speed of development, one thing is for sure – our dependence on robots is only going to increase as we move further into the 21st century.

△ Automata, like this model carriage, are machines that simulate realistic activity.

What is a robot?

There is no one perfect definition of a robot. It is fair to say, however, that it is an automated machine that performs some human-like actions, and reacts to certain external events as well as pre-programmed instructions. A robot does not have to look like a human. Robots are built to designs that are most suited to their work. If a robot is to work in one place, for example, it does not need legs or a system to move around.

△ The Unimate robot is a direct descendant of the very first robot arm – a machine that first handled hot metal die-casting in 1961.

Intelligent glimmers

Early robots were extremely good at repeating an identical operation time and time again. New generations of robots, equipped with high-resolution vision systems and complex object recognition will be able to adjust and adapt to a greater range of work scenarios. By 2030, robots are likely to be equipped with advanced fuzzy logic circuits. These will help them make decisions in keeping with the complexities and problems of the real world.

△ The word 'robot' featured in a 1922 play called *Rossum's Universal Robots,* by Karel Čapek. It comes from the Czech word meaning 'forced labour'.

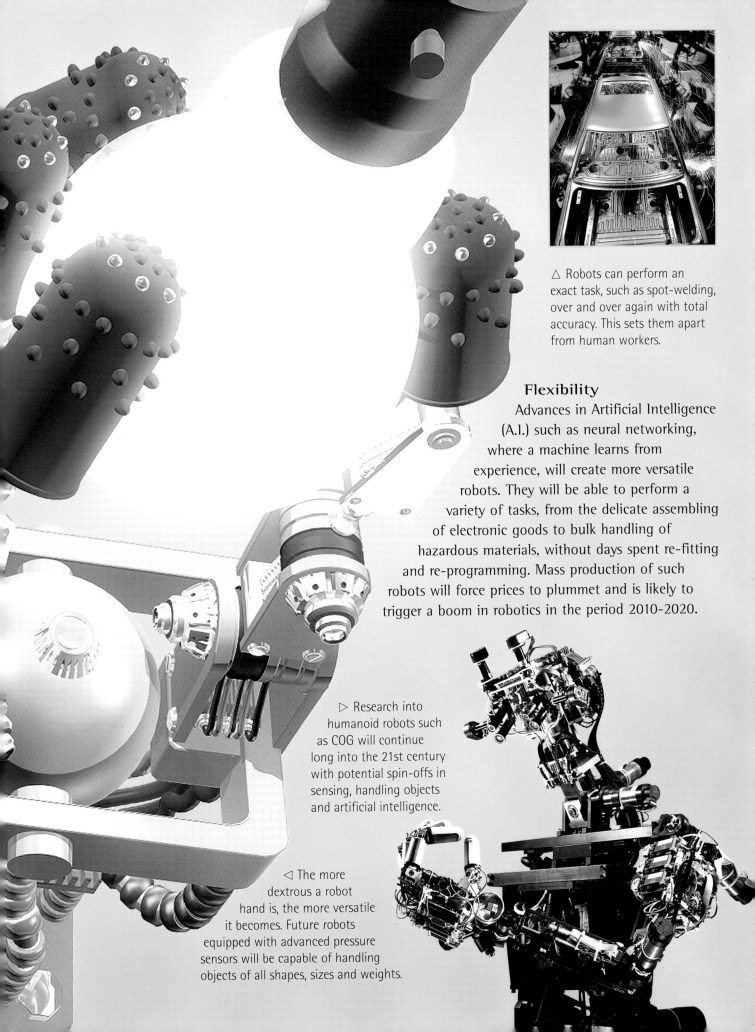

△ Robots can perform an exact task, such as spot-welding, over and over again with total accuracy. This sets them apart from human workers.

Flexibility

Advances in Artificial Intelligence (A.I.) such as neural networking, where a machine learns from experience, will create more versatile robots. They will be able to perform a variety of tasks, from the delicate assembling of electronic goods to bulk handling of hazardous materials, without days spent re-fitting and re-programming. Mass production of such robots will force prices to plummet and is likely to trigger a boom in robotics in the period 2010-2020.

▷ Research into humanoid robots such as COG will continue long into the 21st century with potential spin-offs in sensing, handling objects and artificial intelligence.

◁ The more dextrous a robot hand is, the more versatile it becomes. Future robots equipped with advanced pressure sensors will be capable of handling objects of all shapes, sizes and weights.

SMART FACTORIES

The Industrial Revolution in Europe during the 18th century and 19th century altered the way most people had been working for thousands of years. Time-consuming handiwork by an individual was replaced by factories that grouped together large numbers of people and machinery. During the 20th century, assembly lines, automation and early industrial robots increased productivity and made possible the mass manufacture of affordable products. The smart factory of the 21st century will make products even more easily available and cheaper to buy. Smart factories will depend on advances in artificial intelligence, robotics and automation processes to create factories that can function with almost no human involvement.

△ Working conditions in factories of the 1800s were often dirty, cramped and dangerous. People were forced to perform tedious, repetitive tasks for hours on end.

▷ Automatic guided vehicles (AGVs) transport materials and components between automated processes. Here, an AGV ferries a car shell along an assembly line in Turin, Italy.

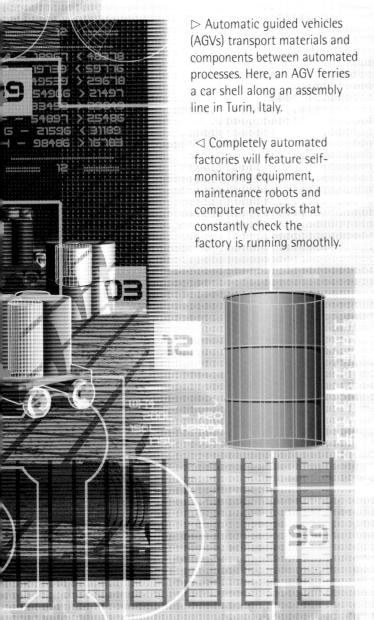

◁ Completely automated factories will feature self-monitoring equipment, maintenance robots and computer networks that constantly check the factory is running smoothly.

Remote factories

By 2030, smart factories will be able to operate with the minimum of human input. These factories will feature self-monitoring equipment, robot maintenance and repair, and a mixture of software and robot supervision. Unlike past factories, they will not need to be located near large towns, which in earlier times would have provided the workforce. Instead, they may be built in remote sites or near raw material sources.

Consumer power

With competition even more intense than in the previous century, 21st-century manufacturers will offer products made in automated factories but indvidually tailored to the customer's needs. Shoppers will be able to customize many products from an extensive list of options. The data will be sent over a computer network to a smart factory that will manufacture and rapidly despatch the product whether it is a vehicle or a new pair of shoes.

Self-assembly

Artificial intelligence developments together with more powerful and accurate sensors are the keys to industrial robot development. As robots become more versatile, their cost will drop. The manufacture of robots, just like other 21st-century products, will benefit from mass production technology. By 2025, they will be built in smart factories by other robots.

BLURRED VISION

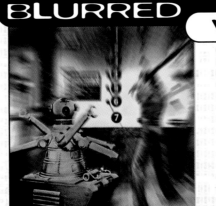

Many people once feared that robots would rebel against their human masters. Instead, robots have become just one of the many automatic features of the advanced factory.

MICRO MACHINES

Machines have been getting smaller and smaller for decades. The arrival of electronic components such as the transistor and integrated circuits have helped shrink many machines to a fraction of their previous size. But miniaturization is not just about shrinking, it is also about packing more functionality into the same size unit. Ballpoint pens, for instance, were once used only for writing. Today, some have a digital clock, radio and voice recorder built in. The driving forces behind miniaturization have come from the needs of various space programmes, the development of new materials and, most importantly, advances in computer technology.

△ Valves used in early electronics were cumbersome and often unreliable. The invention of the transistor in 1947 was a giant step towards the development of micro machinery.

MEMs

MicroElectroMechanical systems, or MEMs for short, are complete machines or components built to the same miniature scale as the circuitry etched onto a silicon chip. Devices from motors and sensing systems the size of a pollen grain to pumps the size of a pinhead could transform engineering in the same way that the silicon chip led to the computer revolution.

▽ Swarms of tiny, cheaply manufactured robot helicopters may be with us by the 2020s. These machines could monitor the condition of crops and selectively get rid of harmful insect pests, without mass spraying of insecticides.

◁ Micro-engineering has produced many scaled-down devices including this working racing car, just 25mm long. The motor that powers the car is only 2.4mm in diameter.

Office on an arm

The building blocks are already in place to construct true portable offices worn as a gauntlet, bracelet or flip-down headset. Processing and memory components are already small enough to be held in the palm of the hand. One problem that remains is the interface between human and machine. Miniature keyboards, for example, are difficult to use. Speech recognition is one solution. One day, direct thought control also may be possible.

△ These micro machine parts are shown next to a fly's leg for scale. Built using similar techniques to the creation of silicon chips, micro motors and machines could be used extensively in industry by 2025.

Working together

Breakthroughs in micro-engineering and robotics will lead to the rise of many-robot systems. These will consist of robots working together in parallel. Together, these machines will be capable of learning from their collective experience in the same way as bees or termites do. As early as 2010, many-robot systems will be performing a variety of tasks such as minesweeping or land surveying.

NANOTECHNOLOGY

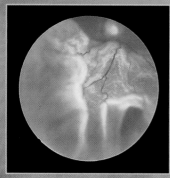

anotechnology is the ultimate in thinking small when it comes to machines. The term comes from the word nanometre, a measurement of one billionth of a metre or the equivalent of about ten atoms long. Nanotechnology is technology and machinery that has been created to this scale. The impact of nanotechnology on almost every area of our lives is potentially limitless. Nano-machines could work within other machines and objects, maintaining them so that they never break down or wear out. Self-repairing car engines and clothing will reduce waste and usher in a new age. According to one nanotechnology expert, Ralph Merkle, "Nanotechnology can be the cornerstone of future technology, a fundamental factor in the future development of civilization."

△ A detached retina is an eye condition that can lead to permanent blindness. By 2060, surgery for this condition, as well as many others, will be transformed by nanotechnology.

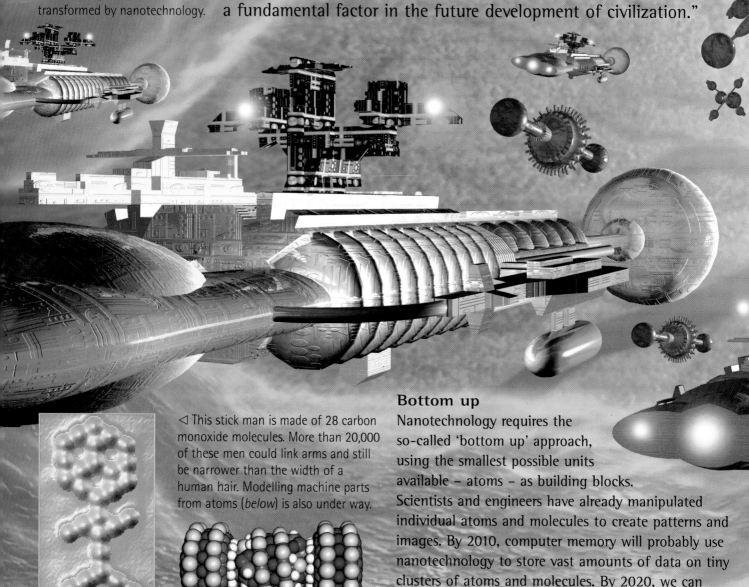

◁ This stick man is made of 28 carbon monoxide molecules. More than 20,000 of these men could link arms and still be narrower than the width of a human hair. Modelling machine parts from atoms (*below*) is also under way.

Bottom up

Nanotechnology requires the so-called 'bottom up' approach, using the smallest possible units available – atoms – as building blocks. Scientists and engineers have already manipulated individual atoms and molecules to create patterns and images. By 2010, computer memory will probably use nanotechnology to store vast amounts of data on tiny clusters of atoms and molecules. By 2020, we can expect the first nano-machines to be manufactured.

Saving the planet

Nanotechnology could create paint for road markings, full of minute solar cells that generate vast amounts of pollution-free electricity from solar power. Smart engines could include nano-machines that reduce polluting waste compounds. Fleets of nano-robots, known as nanobots, created in huge numbers, could be put to work repairing the ozone layer or cleaning up areas of the world polluted by older technology.

Working inside you

One of the most exciting goals of nanotechnology is the creation of nano-machines that can repair our bodies from the inside. This would revolutionize our health. Medical nanobots could enter the bloodstream, scrubbing our blood vessels free of cholesterol and unblocking clogged arteries and veins. Smart toothpaste could even contain fleets of nanobots that detect and remove plaque.

△ At present, oil slicks cause major pollution problems. An army of nanobots could work at a microscopic level, breaking down and reprocessing an oil slick before serious damage is done.

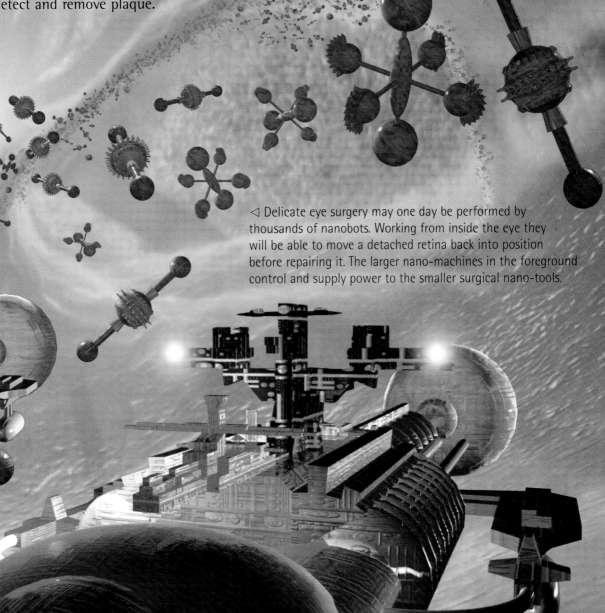

◁ Delicate eye surgery may one day be performed by thousands of nanobots. Working from inside the eye they will be able to move a detached retina back into position before repairing it. The larger nano-machines in the foreground control and supply power to the smaller surgical nano-tools.

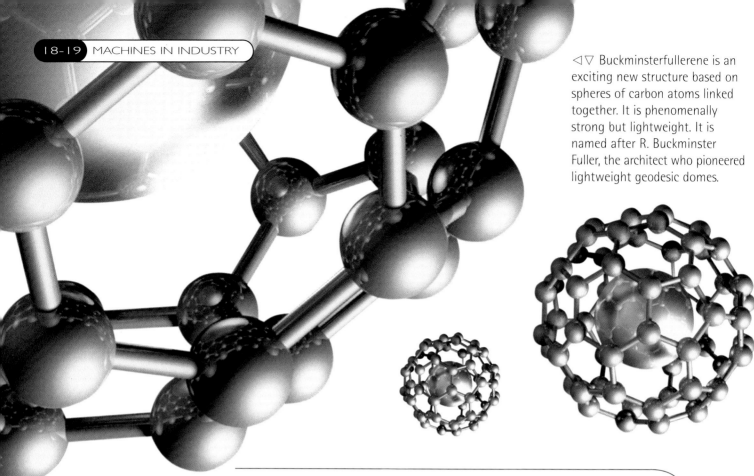

◁▽ Buckminsterfullerene is an exciting new structure based on spheres of carbon atoms linked together. It is phenomenally strong but lightweight. It is named after R. Buckminster Fuller, the architect who pioneered lightweight geodesic domes.

NEW MATERIALS

Humans have always had the urge to create something new from the raw materials found on Earth. From the discovery of metal alloys created by mixing base metals together in the Bronze Age over 4,000 years ago, to the creation of plastics from oil and petroleum, this drive for new materials has helped shape civilization. In the future we can expect to see many new materials or developments of old ones. Some of these materials will offer improvements in areas such as strength, heat-resistance or recyclability. Others will offer radically new and unexpected benefits.

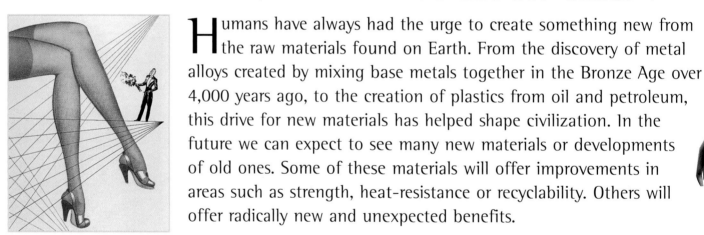

△ Nylon stockings appeared in the early 1940s. They were one of the first products to be developed from processing oil.

Composites

Composite materials are made of several different materials bonded together. Since the early 1970s they have had a huge impact on many machines and products from personal defence armour to spacecraft. Important composite materials include Kevlar, glass-reinforced plastic (GRP), metal matrix composites and carbon-reinforced ceramics.

△ Lycra is a fabric that reduces muscle vibration, a major cause of muscle fatigue. Lycra can help athletes to perform better.

△ At 330x magnification, the individual fibres of fibreglass can be seen clearly. Fibreglass is a strong but lightweight composite material.

Shape memory alloys (SMAs) can remember their original shape and return to it after being stretched or compressed. By the end of the 21st century, homes, offices and other structures built with SMA materials will be capable of withstanding earthquakes.

◁ Spectacles made from shape memory alloys have already been produced. They do not break even after being crumpled and crushed.

Electric threads

Smart materials are able to react and adapt to their environment. They are already found in reactolite sunglasses and 'breathable' fabrics. Electrotextiles is one very exciting area of development. Researchers have created carbon-impregnated fibres that can transmit electric signals. Electrotextiles could be used in nerve-stimulating body suits for people with disabilities or clothes with fully integrated communication systems.

◁ A wide array of electronic devices from computers and communication systems to health monitoring devices will be embedded in electrotextile clothing of the future.

New materials, new possiblities

Computers, airliners and many other 20th-century inventions would not have been possible without plastics, new metal alloys and silicon. New materials in the 21st century will help drive technologies in a similar way. Areas that are likely to benefit from advances in materials include superconductivity, nuclear fusion and virtual reality.

▽ Silica aerogel, developed by NASA, is an almost perfect heat insulator. It is as light as a feather and is likely to have a huge variety of applications from spacecraft to refrigerators.

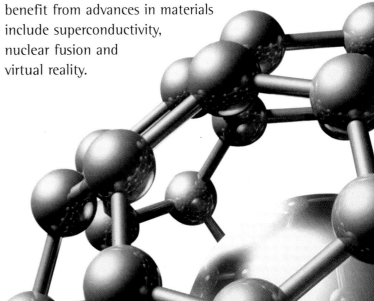

CREATING POWER

Machines have always needed power in order to work. Until the 1800s, most machines, such as bellows or ploughs, only required the muscular effort of humans or animals, while a few, such as waterwheels, were driven by the channelling of simple, natural movement. The advent of electricity and the internal combustion engine changed machines forever. Today, power generating stations, oil refineries and petroleum production sites feed the world's insatiable demand for power. During the 20th century, power consumption increased more than ten times. By the year 2020, world demand for power will have increased again by at least 50 per cent. Many of the fuels used today will not last forever. This fact, together with growing environmental concerns, will lead to a greater emphasis on efficient power production storage and use. Research into potentially vital areas such as superconductivity, nuclear fusion and alternative, renewable energies may lead to a major breakthrough that will help us rely less on traditional fuels for power.

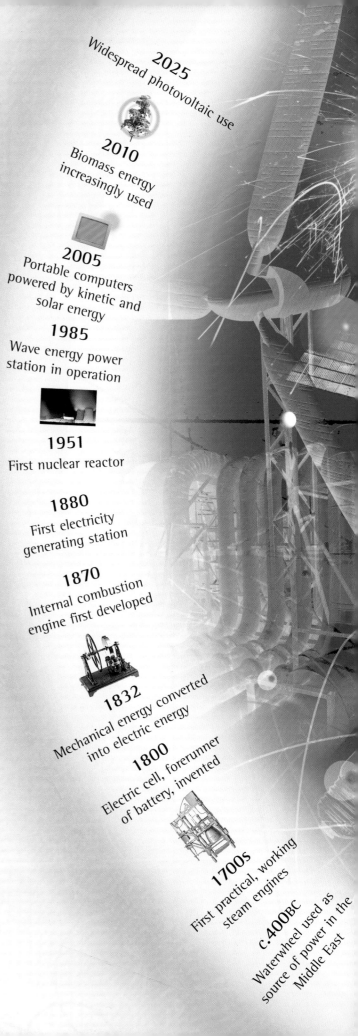

2025
Widespread photovoltaic use

2010
Biomass energy increasingly used

2005
Portable computers powered by kinetic and solar energy

1985
Wave energy power station in operation

1951
First nuclear reactor

1880
First electricity generating station

1870
Internal combustion engine first developed

1832
Mechanical energy converted into electric energy

1800
Electric cell, forerunner of battery, invented

1700s
First practical, working steam engines

c. 400BC
Waterwheel used as source of power in the Middle East

FOSSIL FUELS

Coal, oil and natural gas power the modern world. Formed over millions of years, these fossil fuels are created by layers of sediment and rock that have compressed decaying animal and plant matter. During the early decades of the 21st century, humans will continue to rely on these fossil fuels despite the ecological problems created by their waste gases. Fossil fuels are a finite, non-renewable resource. They will not last forever at the rate we are using them. Stocks are dwindling, although not as fast as predicted in the 1960s and 1970s. Since then, new exploration and extraction techniques have led to the discovery and recovery of previously unknown reserves.

△ Our great need for coal and oil has resulted in massive mining operations all over the world such as this open-cast mine in Germany. The demand for fossil fuels will continue for many decades to come.

◁ One alternative to petrol is bio-fuel, which is made from processing certain plants. Improvements in extraction may lead to much more widespread use of bio-fuel.

△ Connah's Quay gas-fired power station in North Wales uses an advanced system called combined cycle gas turbine (CCGT). It is 40 per cent more efficient than a regular coal-fired station.

Remote operation

Even with advances in solar power and other alternative energies, fossil fuels will still be required both as a fuel and as a raw material for plastics and other substances. The search for new reserves, from 2015 onwards, will be conducted by a new generation of robots and intelligent machines. By 2030, remote ocean mining and drilling will take place in many parts of the world. Drilling rigs and coal mines will also be operated remotely in inhospitable areas, such as deserts.

Nightmare scenario

The dwindling of fossil fuels will have a major impact on the planet. We are dependent on machines – many of which rely on fossil fuels to make them work. No power means no machines and society would grind to a halt. Even a major rise in fuel prices could lead to a catastrophic world recession because the economy is directly linked to the price of these vital substances. The search for alternative energy sources will become more and more important during the 21st century.

More efficiency

With the world demand for electricity expected to double by 2020, there will be major efforts to make more efficient use of fossil fuels in the 21st century. One way to achieve this is to improve the way we store electricity and transmit it. Maintaining power lines will become vital and by 2015, we can expect to see special power line robots working more quickly, safely and efficiently than their human counterparts.

◁ Core samples taken from the arctic wastelands, or tundra, have indicated great reserves of oil and gas. By 2025, remote automated drilling platforms may be built here. They will require only rare maintenance visits from human personnel.

The search for fuels and other resources may eventually lead to exploration and mining of bodies other than the Earth. By 2100, mining units might recover ore from the Moon and asteroids. The ore will be reprocessed into high-grade fuel and then transported back to Earth.

▽△ By 2018, maintenance robots powered by fans and small air thrusters will hover around power lines. Armed with gripping and cutting tools, they will monitor a line's condition and perform repairs.

ENERGY FROM ATOMS

△ Calder Hall was Britain's first nuclear power station. It began generating electricity in 1956 and is still operational today.

Splitting atoms, a process called nuclear fission, generates previously unimagined amounts of power without using up fossil fuel stocks. However, nuclear power does have major disadvantages. The high levels of radioactivity generated are a potentially lethal health risk. There are also enormous costs involved in safeguarding against such risks and dealing with radioactive waste. Nuclear power development is slow at present but, if fossil fuel stocks dwindle and global warming fears increase, it is possible that in the 21st century nuclear power will take a dominant position as a power producer.

Public image

Nuclear power produces very little of the polluting gases that cause acid rain or global warming. However, unlike many technologies in the 21st century, nuclear power will have to overcome negative public opinion. Confidence in nuclear power took a sharp downturn after incidents such as the 1986 Chernobyl disaster in the Ukraine and the continuing concerns over waste disposal. Scientists will continue to work to reduce the risks and develop safer nuclear power.

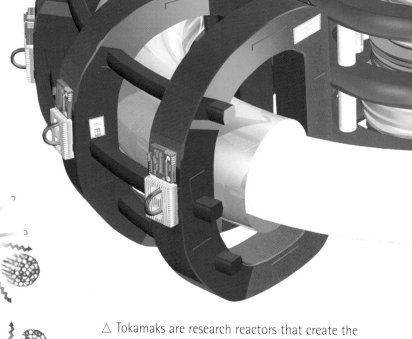

△ Tokamaks are research reactors that create the extreme temperatures required for nuclear fusion. They use a doughnut-shaped arrangement of powerful electromagnets, along with high-energy particle beams.

◁ In nuclear fission, a neutron collides with an unstable U-235 atom, causing it to split. This releases more neutrons and a great deal of energy. With more U-235 atoms present, this sets off a chain reaction.

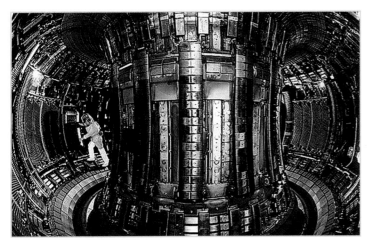

△ This tokamak fusion reactor is part of the Joint European Torus project in England. Others research establishments use lasers to generate the heat required.

△ Fast-breeder reactors, like Dounreay in Scotland, can produce up to 60 times the energy of a regular nuclear fission reactor. However, there are still technological problems and high costs.

Waste disposal

The disposal of high-level radioactive waste created by the nuclear power process is a huge problem. The waste has to be stored for as long as 10,000 years before its radioactivity falls to harmless levels. Most of the world's nuclear waste is in temporary storage facilities awaiting decisions on its fate. By 2010, permanent facilities for ultra-long-term storage will have to be established despite the fierce public debate their siting will provoke.

▷ Vitrification fixes radioactive waste in an inert glass or ceramic compound. It is then encased in a heavy, metal cannister prior to underground burial.

The holy grail

In the process of nuclear fusion, heavy hydrogen atoms join together to form helium in a self-sustaining reaction that produces enormous amounts of energy. However, this only occurs at temperatures of millions of degrees centigrade. Scientists are developing different ways of heating atoms to these levels and building a container that can safely handle such temperatures. Whether the goal of safe and unlimited commercial nuclear fusion is a possibility is a question unlikely to be answered until the middle of the 21st century.

BLURRED VISION

In the 1930s, nuclear power promised a golden age of cheap, clean, limitless energy. By the mid-1950s, when nuclear power stations were first built, long-term waste storage and fears of contamination were major issues.

ENERGY
FROM THE CORES

Nuclear fusion has provided the Earth with energy for billions of years. Nuclear fusion is behind the Sun's awesome power. However, the fraction of the Sun's output that reaches Earth is a staggering 30,000 times more than the energy we actually use. This incredible resource will give us sustainable, pollution-free power if scientists learn to tap it more efficiently. Although it is dwarfed in comparison to the Sun's energy, the Earth's core also generates considerable heat. Work will continue to progress on geothermal technologies that will harness some of this heat energy and convert it into electrical power. In the future it is likely to increase in importance as an additional pollution-free energy supply.

△ The technology behind generating solar power is not new. This solar cooker, which boils the water in a coffee-pot, dates back to the 1960s.

△ Solar-powered calculators have been available since the 1970s. They use photovoltaic cells to convert sunlight into electrical power.

Solar heat
One form of solar power generation makes use of the Sun's warming energy. It uses solar heat reflectors to gather in the Sun's heat and focus it on a collector. Heat collectors work like radiators in reverse – they collect the heat that is used to boil a liquid such as oil or water. In the case of water, the steam that is created drives electricity-generating turbines.

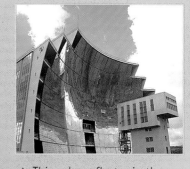

△ This solar reflector in the Pyrenees in France is made up of 9,500 mirrors and automatically turns to track the Sun.

Sunlight power
Light energy from the Sun can also generate solar power. Photovoltaic cells consist of two layers. When the light strikes the top layer of cells, it knocks electrons free from their atoms.
These electrons move between the two layers, helping to generate an electric current.
As photovoltaic cells become more efficient and cheaper to manufacture, a boom in solar power is likely to occur. In the coming years, photovoltaic cells will be fitted to cars, buildings and even clothing, where they could power lightweight electronic devices.

△ Honda's solar-powered research vehicle may be the forerunner of solar vehicles found on the road by the 2020s.

Hot rocks

Geothermal power comes from energy under the Earth's surface that heats water. This water is either used to supply heating and hot water to nearby homes and factories, or it is pumped through a heat exchanger. This converts it into steam that is used to drive electricity generators. From 2020 onwards, geothermal power stations will become more common, as breakthroughs in drilling deeper into the Earth and the use of Hot Dry Rock (HDR) technology make it possible to build geothermal stations in many more locations.

△ Icelandic bathers enjoy the hot water generated by a geothermal power station. These power stations are sited in areas of intense thermal activity.

△ Future geothermal power stations may be completely automatic and located in areas of great thermal, or even volcanic, activity. They will be remote controlled from a distance by human technicians. Maintenance robots and machines will monitor and make routine repairs.

▽ Each panel of this solar power station consists of thousands of solar cells and a grid of metal conductors that together turn sunlight into an electrical current.

HARNESSING THE ELEMENTS

Fears that fossil fuel supplies were running low and concerns about the damage caused by their emissions led to much research in the late 20th century on alternative, low-pollution forms of power. Nature provides us with potential energy sources that are endless even if they are not constant. The movement of wind, wave and tides all can be turned into useful energy. In the 21st century, scientists and engineers will work on creating efficient, cost-effective energy generation from wind and water. A major breakthrough will make a huge difference in the ways future generations obtain power.

△ The mechanical power created by waterwheels has been used for centuries to grind corn and pump water.

△ The first tidal power station was built in France across the River Rance. It has been in operation since 1966.

Water power

Hydroelectric power (HEP) uses the force of water flowing downwards to turn turbines that generate electricity. Different types of turbine are used for different geographical locations. The largest current scheme is at Itaipu on the Brazil–Paraguay border and it generates 10,000 megawatts of power. Research into new, more efficient types of turbine will result in a number of hydroelectric projects across the globe exceeding this power-generating figure by 2015.

▽ Offshore wind farms could be a feature of many coastlines in the future. Denmark is leading the way. By 2030, it is estimated that more than 25 per cent of all Denmark's electricity will be generated by offshore wind farms.

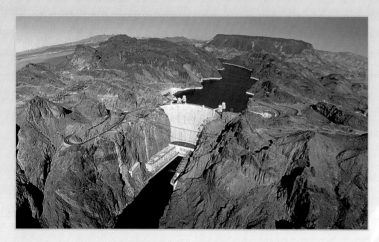

△ Mountainous locations and large dams, such as the Hoover Dam in Arizona, US, provide a fast-flowing water source needed to make a hydroelectric scheme effective.

Farming the wind

Wind power spins a wind turbine's blades which cause a generator to turn and create electricity. As materials and low-friction design technologies are developed, wind turbines will increase in efficiency. Sited together in large numbers on open land, hill-tops and even offshore, wind farms are likely to become an increasingly important source of efficient energy. Even so, there are still concerns over their environmental impact, as wind farms are noisy and affect the view.

◁ The blades of this experimental Vertical Axis Wind Turbine allow it to work regardless of wind direction.

Waves and tides

Since ancient times, the power of the waves and tides of the seas and oceans has inspired awe in many people. The prospect of harnessing this power has excited many researchers. However, the major obstacle is the size and cost of physical structures that stretch across rivers, estuaries and seas. By the year 2025, even though a number of tidal and wave power stations may be in operation, they are likely to be overshadowed by massive increases in wind and solar power generation.

◁ The first battery was invented in 1800 by the Italian scientist Alessandro Volta and was called a voltaic pile. It consisted of discs of copper, zinc and card saturated with a salt solution.

▽ A technique called computational fluid dynamics (CFD) allows computers to map accurately the effects of gases and liquids around an object such as this space plane. CFD helps scientists cut down friction and other energy waste.

GREATER EFFICIENCY

Once a machine is invented, people have usually tried to improve its efficiency – to make it do more for less power. This will become even more important in the future – especially with growing concerns over the effects of certain forms of power on the environment. Scientists and engineers are researching new ways of getting more for less by improving design, streamlining and using advanced materials. Greater efficiency is a goal for all future machines – not just the electronic and mechanical machines and the vehicles that consume power, but also the power stations and transmission devices that generate power in the first place.

◁ A combination of lightweight composite materials and an enhanced streamlined design are behind the incredible performance of this record-breaking racing bike.

Electric power

Power stations in the early years of the 21st century will be able to produce electricity with less fuel than is currently used. At the same time, improved technology will transmit the electricity to homes, offices and factories more efficiently. Portable electricity storage is also likely to improve. The super-batteries of the 2020s will store far more electricity than today's. Many more batteries will be rechargeable and easier to recycle.

The idea of a perpetual motion machine, which generates enough power, once started, to keep running forever, has occupied many scientists over the centuries. It is now believed that such a machine goes against the laws of physics.

▷ The Japanese Magnetic Levitation (Maglev) train uses powerful electric magnets to raise the train just above the track. The massive reduction in friction results in a faster, more efficient train.

Electricity without energy loss

The ability of certain materials to conduct electricity at incredibly low temperatures with no resistance or power loss is called superconductivity. A great deal of research is still needed to develop superconducting materials that are practical to shape and use, and that work at less extreme temperatures. By 2030, we should begin to see superconductors in extremely efficient electric motors and in power lines that can transmit electricity for hundreds of kilometres without energy loss.

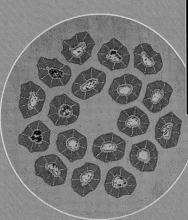

◁△ YBCO is a ceramic superconductor that works at relatively high temperatures. It allows electricity to be conducted without resistance.

A lack of friction

Friction – the resistance caused by two things rubbing together – creates wear and heat, and reduces the performance of many machines. Research into ways of minimizing friction will continue far into the 21st century. Advances are likely to be made in more effective lubrication systems, greater use of computer modelling to improve steamlining and the creation of new materials that will generate very little friction.

MILITARY MACHINES

Conflict and warfare have always been a feature of human societies. Sticks and stones, wielded in the hand or thrown, provided some of the earliest weapons. Gradually, methods were developed to propel weapons across greater distances and with more force, from the slingshot and crossbow to cannons, firearms and torpedoes. Advances in weapons' development reached a new stage in the 20th century when the human race had the capability to destroy life on the planet many times over. With this terrifying capacity came a new responsibility to prevent a Third World War occurring. Conflict will still exist, however, in the 21st century. Terrorism and localized warfare will continue as various groups jostle for superiority in increasingly fractured territories. In this complex future world, where enemies are more and more difficult to pinpoint, the need for up-to-the-minute information will increase as will rapid strike forces and unmanned, autonomous weaponry and systems.

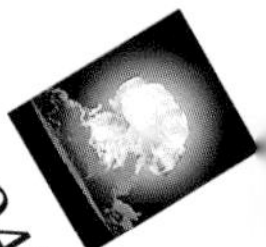

1945
Atomic bomb detonated

1944
First jet aircraft flown in combat

1916
Tanks first used in World War I

1911
First military aircraft used for reconnaissance

1864
First self-propelled torpedo

1835
First revolver

1300s
Cannons used in warfare

AD600s
Gunpowder invented

2030
Anti-satellite
weapons
deployed

2025
Incendiary robots in
sabotage operation

1983
Stealth fighters and
bombers in service

SPYING AND DEFENCE

Ever since wars began, opposing sides have attempted to find out as much as they can about the enemy's position, size and weaponry. Spying has always involved sending human scouts and agents behind enemy lines. However, in the future we are likely to see unmanned machines taking over, with human operatives safely conducting surveillance operations at a distance over computer networks. Advances in information technology will mean that a person's actions over the Internet and other networks will be traced easily. By 2010, electronic tagging by mini-transmitter may also provide accurate tracking of individuals without their knowledge.

△▽ Cameras have long been used for spying, often hidden in household items or miniaturized to make them harder to detect. Advances in micro-engineering will continue to shrink the size of radios, bugs and cameras – the tools of the spy's trade.

Stealth

"See but not be seen" is a motto for all spies and especially for pilots of spy and reconnaissance aircraft flying over enemy territory. Stealth technology is designed to confuse enemy radar and other sensors and allow aircraft to fly undetected and unopposed. Featuring radar-absorbing paints, angled facets and low-heat emitting engines, this technology is being improved for the second generation of stealth planes and is also being adapted to land and sea vehicles.

△ Spy films like the famous James Bond series tend to show agents operating in isolation. In reality, many spies work in close contact with their controllers.

△▷ The minimum size of an object seen from a spy satellite is known as its resolution. Current satellites are believed to have a resolution of half a metre or less. Future models will be able to read over a person's shoulder, if they are not already capable of doing so.

Spies in the sky

Despite the effectiveness of stealth technology, pilots and crew will continue to remain at risk. One viable alternative is automated, computer-controlled pilotless aircraft. Pilotless drones have already been used for some routine duties but as computer control becomes more sophisticated, unmanned aerial vehicles (UAVs) will increasingly fly missions over enemy territory. By 2015, many reconnaissance and spying flights will be performed by UAVs.

Spying from space

It is no secret that many of the satellites orbiting Earth are used for spying. What is secret, however, is the definition and quality of the images. The results that the public sees are probably not the very best that intelligence agencies can obtain. Satellites are used because they provide relatively risk-free information gathering. However, this may not always be the case. NASA and the Pentagon are currently spending $50 million a year on developing anti-spy satellite devices.

△ The Lockheed *B2* bomber has a stealth flying wing design covered in radar-absorbing materials. These enable it to fly deep into enemy territory without detection.

◁ Everything a spy needs to conduct video surveillance can be contained in a briefcase. Remote-operated machines may perform this sort of surveillance task by 2020.

PERSONAL WEAPONS

Until the discovery of gunpowder in the 10th century, most personal weapons, such as spears and swords, relied on human muscle power. With the application of gunpowder people began to use artificially-powered weapons such as cannons, muskets and later, machine guns and revolvers. These worked over far greater distances than previous weapons and were much more lethal. In the first half of the 21st century, firearms will be similar to those of the late 20th century. The main differences will be in how the new weapons are targeted and the ways in which people can be protected from their destructive effects.

△ Rapid-firing machine-guns such as the *Maxim Mk1*, designed in 1884, considerably changed the nature of warfare.

Invention then protection

Weapons development goes through a cycle of invention then protection. As soon as a weapon is created, efforts are made to protect against it. By 2010, when even the smallest handgun will pack a lethal punch, more effective and lightweight body armour will be developed that uses blends of new composites and other materials. By 2030, some armour may offer stealth capablilities or provide power in the form of solar cells built into the outer shell.

▷ Members of the French Special Police Force are equipped with body armour and image-intensifying goggles.

△ This body armour, constructed out of woven meshes of steel and composites, such as Kevlar, can withstand a bullet fired even at short range.

◁ By 2015, many guns will use microprocessors to detect a permitted user's electronic signature before the safety catch is unlocked. Alternative safety devices may scan the palm and fingerprints of the hand holding the weapon.

Battles without bullets

Lethal personal weapons that do not use bullets may be a very real threat by 2020. These weapons will use concentrated toxic gas sprays, light beams or sound focused at a high frequency to inflict harm. Many major military powers are already researching ways to counter such possible threats. The threat of chemical and biological warfare is also likely to remain, and efforts will be focused on developing fail-safe methods of detection as well as effective antidotes.

△ The *S.I.G.* assault rifle is equipped with an advanced sighting mechanism that uses a laser for pinpoint accuracy.

◁ The sticky shocker projectile administers an electric shock that stuns and temporarily disables the target.

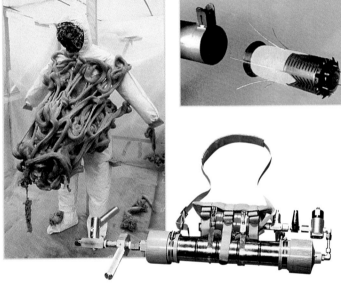

△ The sticky foam gun fires large quantities of highly adhesive foam which stops a target from moving or reaching for a weapon.

Non-lethal weaponry

By 2015, many security and police forces will be equipped with effective non-lethal weaponry that stuns or temporarily disables a target. Weapons being developed include sticky guns and sticky stunners. Sticky guns fire a mass of disabling adhesive foam preventing an individual's escape. Sticky stunners fire a soft-barbed or glue-covered projectile. When they hit a target they administer a disabling electric shock.

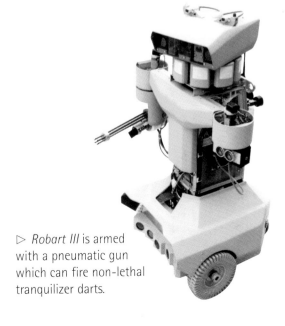

▷ *Robart III* is armed with a pneumatic gun which can fire non-lethal tranquilizer darts.

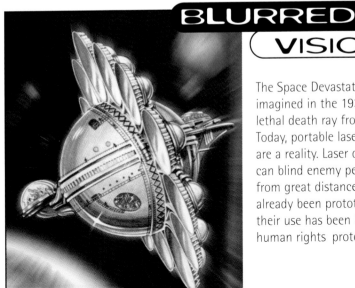

BLURRED VISION

The Space Devastator, as imagined in the 1930s, fired a lethal death ray from space. Today, portable laser weapons are a reality. Laser dazers which can blind enemy personnel from great distances have already been prototyped but their use has been banned by human rights protocols.

◁ The Joint Strike Fighter, in service from 2012, will be a high-performance, multi-role fighter with stealth technology. It will have the ability to climb one kilometre in five seconds.

Delivery systems are the part of military force that deliver weapons to their target. Tanks, aircraft, battleships and submarines were all potent delivery systems in the late 20th century.

DELIVERY SYSTEMS

Some methods of attack, such as rapid air strikes, will increase in importance throughout the 21st century while the role of others such as bomber aircraft and battleships will diminish. Unmanned delivery systems are likely to overtake traditional systems by the middle of the 21st century.

△ The aircraft of Baron von Richtofen's so-called 'flying circus' were a formidable force during World War I. Combat, or dogfights, between enemy aircraft took place at very close range.

▷ These single-mission robot insects, no bigger than a compact disc, will be dropped from the air or deployed from land vehicles. Cheap to produce, they will be launched in large numbers and carry small but highly concentrated explosive charges.

Downsizing

Flagship forces such as unwieldy battle cruisers, massed land battalions and aircraft carriers are likely to be kept on by the major powers for their deterrent effect. However, the role of striking at enemy targets will probably be taken over by swifter, smaller and more accurate delivery systems in the air and on and under the water. Many of these systems will be equipped with stealth technology to avoid detection.

Missiles and smart bombs

The power of unmanned delivery systems has been apparent ever since the German *V1* and *V2* rockets were used during World War II. In the 21st century, we can expect unmanned air machines such as fighters and bombers in action as well as 'smarter' missiles. These unmanned airborne delivery systems will be able to perform manoeuvres, reach targets and take risks that are unsuitable for humans in the cockpit.

△ Smart bombs with on-board navigation sensors were used to deadly effect by the Allied forces in the Gulf War of 1991.

△ Stealth technology is being developed for land and sea machines to make them almost undetectable by enemy radar.

Access all areas

Unmanned delivery systems will not be restricted to airborne devices. Robotic delivery systems will also be developed that work underwater and in all kinds of terrain. Likely advances in robotics by 2025 will allow the relatively cheap manufacture and deployment of robot incendiary devices based on an insect design. These will be ideal for scuttling over difficult terrain before detonating on reaching their target.

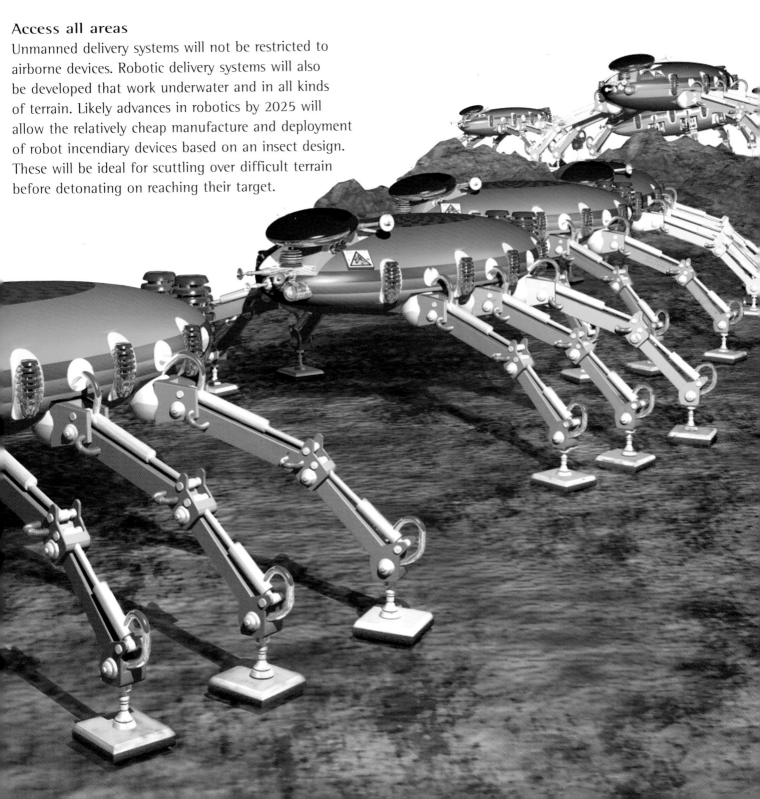

FUTURE BATTLEGROUNDS

△ Static lines of trenches were a feature of World War I. Loss of life was great from constant bombardment and disease.

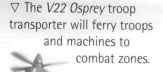

▽ The *V22 Osprey* troop transporter will ferry troops and machines to combat zones.

Until World War II, most major conflicts involved established lines of infantry, cavalry or motorized vehicles moving slowly and painfully forward to engage in massive pitched battles. The success of the highly mobile *Blitzkreig* ('Lightning War'), in the early stages of World War II, shattered the static nature of battles forever. Military conflicts of the future are likely to be small-scale and fought in small areas. They will call on a military force's advanced communications systems as well as its capability to get machines and personnel to the conflict zone as quickly and stealthily as possible.

Rapid response

Small-scale, unexpected and fast-changing conflicts mean the military forces of tomorrow will need to be highly mobile and capable of deployment in hours rather than weeks. Future conflicts will see a machine-led approach with unmanned scout vehicles and tilt-rotor aircraft that can hover to load and unload troops.

△ Command centres in the 21st century will rely on advanced communications systems to control forces.

△ Night vision goggles will become standard equipment for elite troops of the future.

Elite forces

By 2020, the most advanced military powers will be phasing out big battalions of troops in favour of two distinct types of soldier – peacekeeping forces used alongside, or instead of, the police to quell civil unrest, and highly-trained elite forces. Elite forces will be small in number and very mobile. They will be in two-way communication with command centres from where the tactical and organizational war will be fought.

Smart fighters

Elite troops will be equipped to operate alone or in small groups. In addition to two-way radio and data links, they will also be equipped with body-monitoring equipment and night vision goggles. Smart uniforms will incorporate body armour and may have the ability to change camouflage pattern to suit the surroundings.

△ The latest battlewear already incorporates bulletproof visors. Future visors will feature displays projecting information such as mission data or battle status.

▽ By 2030, elite troops will be working with robot infantry. Minute sensors, dropped over the battlefield, will send back vital information to the command centre.

2040
Space hotels in operation

2012
Fully automated stores
with robot assistants

MACHINES
NEAR AND FAR

Many machines, from the winch used at a water well to weapons such as the cannon, were designed to extend the range of a person's actions. This trend continued throughout the 20th century but with one important advance – machines were created which could also be operated by remote control, particularly in dangerous places such as nuclear power stations. Sophisticated communications and control systems allow tele-operated machines to be controlled by operators situated a great distance away. Automation is another important development. Automatic machines and robots with basic intelligence are taking over many day-to-day tasks that were once performed by humans. Automated machines are also working far from home, exploring space and the planets of our Solar System.

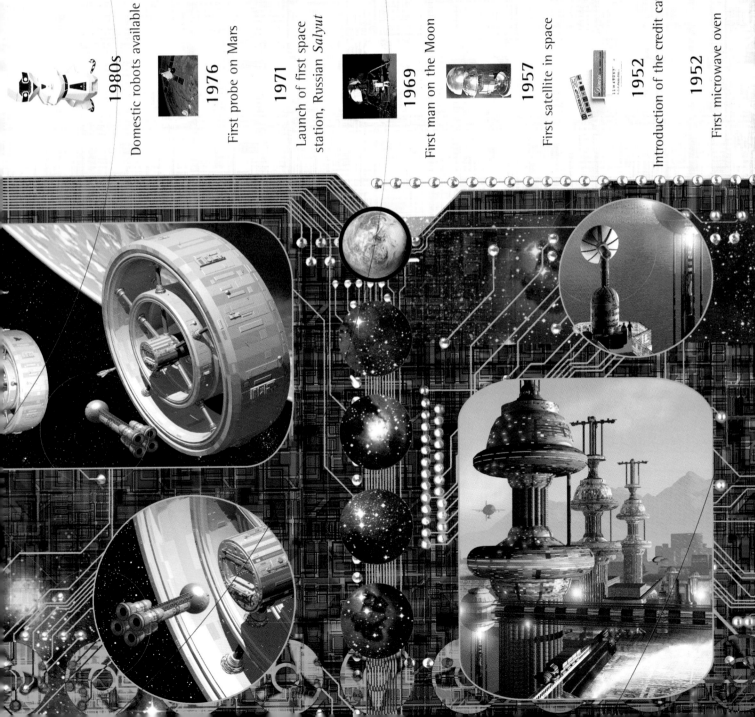

1980s
Domestic robots available

1976
First probe on Mars

1971
Launch of first space
station, Russian *Salyut*

1969
First man on the Moon

1957
First satellite in space

1952
Introduction of the credit card

1952
First microwave oven

IN THE HOME

△ The microwave oven, which cuts down cooking times for many meals, was hailed as the ultimate in labour-saving devices when it was first launched in the 1950s.

During the 20th century many machines, from washing machines to food processors, were designed to cut down the time spent on household chores. New machines in future homes will work even harder for human inhabitants. As the cost of microprocessors continues to plummet, more and more homes will be controlled by computer networks and a fully programmable series of intelligent electronic functions. These will be built into the house during construction and include full security systems, climate and environmental control and advanced telecommunications features.

No cord accord

Wireless power networks will be found in many high-tech homes built after 2015. Most of the electricity required by the network will come from conventional sources but some will be generated by a home's own solar panels. Many electrical devices, from irons to televisions, will be powered by advanced, super-efficient batteries ensuring cable-free operation. Plug sockets will be replaced by recharging stations for these batteries.

Faster food

Advances in food technology and biotechnology will make washing, cutting and peeling fresh foods a thing of the past. Kitchens will eventually be little more than a place where food can be stored, heated and served. Even so, pots, pans and chopping boards will not disappear completely. Some people will still prefer to keep the human touch when cooking food.

△ Intelligent kitchens, such as this research model in Seattle, US, will be standard in homes from 2020. They will feature smart cookers that scan cooking data imprinted on food and apply the correct amount of heat for the right amount of time.

◁ The intelligent rubbish bin uses magnets and material sensors to sort out different types of rubbish for recycling.

CRYSTAL BALL

By 2040, conventional carpet cleaning – either by robots or humans – may be a thing of the past. Electronically controlled carpet fibres could ferry dust and debris to the edge of the carpet where it would be collected in easy-to-empty receptacles.

△ By 2020, pans made from smart metal alloys will be able to sense and adjust exactly how much heat they conduct. This will help them prevent, for example, water or a sauce from boiling over.

Environmental control

Many machines fitted in homes of the future will adjust and monitor different aspects of the environment. Energy conservation will continue to be an important issue. To ensure efficiency, intelligent heating monitors will be found around the house. These will automatically adjust temperatures and be linked to electro-mechanical devices that open and shut windows and doors in order to reduce the energy used in heating or cooling.

▽▷ Smart glass will be able to measure the amount and intensity of light passing through it and automatically dim the glass if the light is too bright.

DOMESTIC ROBOTS

△ This robot lawnmower is solar-powered and has simple collision detectors and sensors that keep the mower within its programmed area.

By 2015, it is estimated that there will be at least three million robots at work in industry. Apart from factories, robots will also be appearing in places such as supermarkets, as security guards and as carers and helpers in hospitals. By 2025, office robots and automatic machines will be handling many mundane tasks now performed by people, for example inputting data and handling phone calls. A new generation of home robots also will be developed. Unlike the novelty toy robots of the 1990s or the one-function machines of 2000–2010, these will be truly versatile robots capable of carrying out a wide variety of tasks.

△ Voice-activated toy robots are the starting-point for educational robots for young children. Robot home tutors will appear in homes from around 2010 onwards.

Home help

Some domestic robots are likely to function as carers for the old, the sick and the disabled. Robot carers, unlike their human counterparts, will not need to take time off for their own lives and will be able to offer 24-hour care and assistance. They will monitor a home patient's medical condition and send back data over a computer network to doctors in a hospital or medical practice.

Early learning

Robotic home tutors will provide one-to-one teaching for many young children in the future. Using artificial intelligence, these robots will perform a range of tasks and activities. Robot tutors will help children acquire early learning skills from basic shape and colour recognition to counting, reading and writing.

▷ The robot assistant of 2030 will have a lightweight robot arm for some physical chores. Most of its work, however, will be conducted over computer networks. It will communicate directly with these networks via a probe that fits into a special wall socket or by using wireless communications systems.

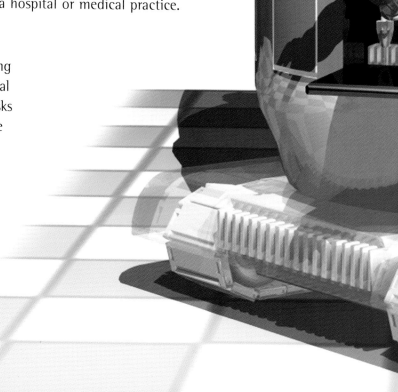

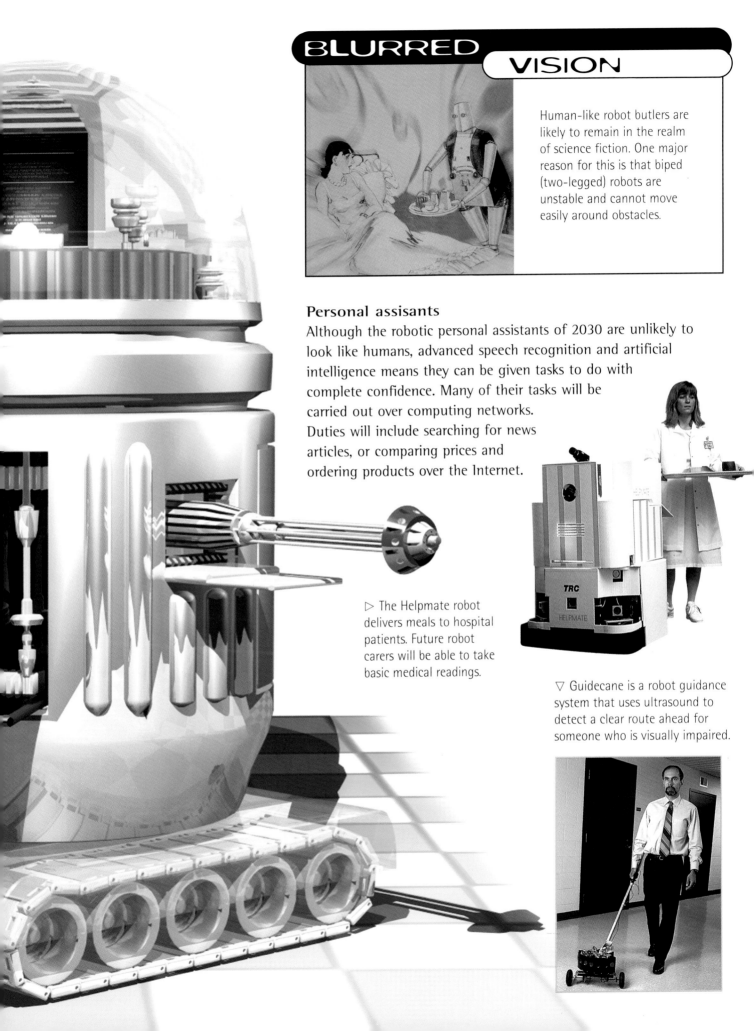

Human-like robot butlers are likely to remain in the realm of science fiction. One major reason for this is that biped (two-legged) robots are unstable and cannot move easily around obstacles.

Personal assisants

Although the robotic personal assistants of 2030 are unlikely to look like humans, advanced speech recognition and artificial intelligence means they can be given tasks to do with complete confidence. Many of their tasks will be carried out over computing networks. Duties will include searching for news articles, or comparing prices and ordering products over the Internet.

▷ The Helpmate robot delivers meals to hospital patients. Future robot carers will be able to take basic medical readings.

▽ Guidecane is a robot guidance system that uses ultrasound to detect a clear route ahead for someone who is visually impaired.

▷ Before computers, banking was slow, time-consuming and relied on sifting through vast amounts of paper records.

SHOPPING AND BANKING

Shopping, banking and security will change dramatically during the 21st century. In the late 20th century many communities had already moved towards electronic currency. Electronic money – in the form of microprocessors holding a person's complete financial details – will eventually replace paper and coin money. Electronic currency and the growth of the Net for shopping will mean that financial transactions will be handled only by machines. This will create a need for accurate verification of a person's identity. Security systems are most likely to be based on biometrics – the scientific measurement of an individual's physical features.

Biometrics

Biometrics is expected to become one of the fastest-growing industries in the first half of the 21st century. Biometrics uses the unique characteristics of the human voice or a particular part of the body – the face, finger, ear or eye, for example, to identify someone. A biometric system scans one or more of these features and then looks for a match, comparing the information with what is held in its memory.

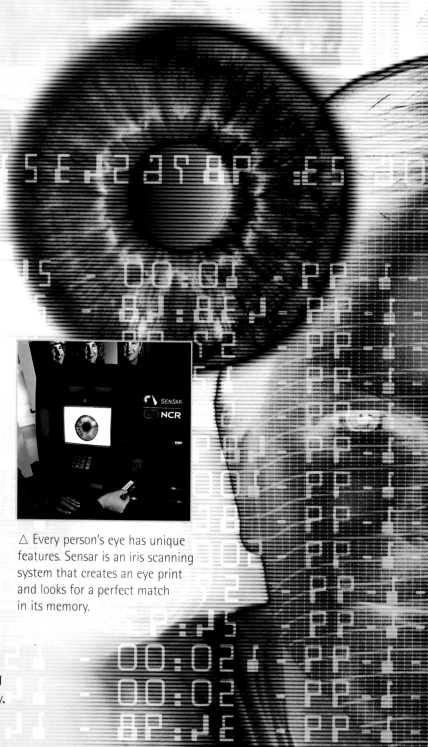

△ Every person's eye has unique features. Sensar is an iris scanning system that creates an eye print and looks for a perfect match in its memory.

Wallet replacement

How will the new electronic currencies be carried? The majority of our credit and financial details will be held in automatic machines that can be accessed via a biometric security system. Microprocessors fitted to a smart card or even implanted within the body could hold financial records. These devices would also be capable of performing functions such as instant currency conversion.

△ At the end of the 20th century, shopping over the Internet was still in its early stages. With improved security and virtual reality systems, shopping from home or local VR stations is expected to flourish by 2010.

△ This robot shopping trolley uses ultrasound to follow a customer around the world's first automated department store, Seibu, in Japan.

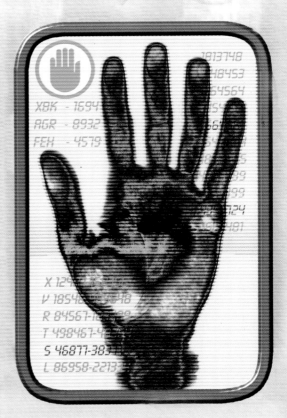

△ Electronic hand scanners could be in widespread use in many countries by 2010.

◁ A user's eye is scanned by an automatic teller machine (ATM) of 2015. A cross-reference check with other aspects of the face or via a hand scanner may be run before the user is allowed access to funds or account information.

Watching you

Like it or not, in the 21st century our lives may be constantly monitored and many of our actions recorded. Internet, credit card and smartcard tracking as well as the growth in advanced digital camera systems and closed-circuit TV (CCTV) surveillance will mean that many parts of our lives will be monitored. In the future a major public movement is likely to be concerned with campaigning for less intrusion and more privacy.

MACHINES IN HAZARDOUS AREAS

Machines are ideally suited to performing dangerous jobs or working in hazardous places. Machines have already travelled to distant and hostile planets and explored the ocean depths where no humans could survive. On land, machines perform jobs that we cannot do and in places that we cannot visit. Such no-go areas include sites where toxic chemicals and radioactivity are present, the insides of storage tanks and pipelines, and in and around active volcanoes or fierce fires where the heat is intense. As the 21st century progresses, sophisticated hazard robots, or hazbots, will be constructed from materials that are resistant to heat, shock and other dangers.

△ A bomb disposal robot approaches a bomb. It has a long-reaching robot arm with various tools for defusing bombs and controlling explosions.

Defusing the situation

One legacy of previous military conflicts is that unexploded mines, bombs and shells (together known as ordnance) are littered all over the world. With a rise in terrorism predicted, bomb disposal robots will be called upon increasingly for fast and safe defusing and disposal of unexploded ordnance. Many of these specialized robots will be tele-operated by a human controller positioned a safe distance away.

▷ Future fire-fighting robots will use visual signals and sounds to lead people to escape exits. They will also provide oxygen masks, and spray water and other flame-extinguishing substances to cut a protective path through the fire.

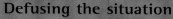

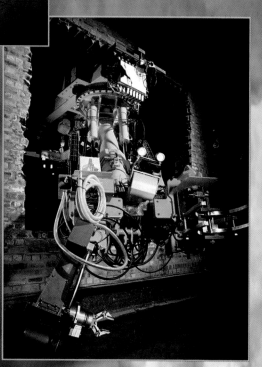

◁ Remote-controlled robot arms are commonplace in the nuclear industry. The human operator uses hand controls to move the robot's arms. The robot, which is not affected by radiation, can make very precise movements.

Nuclear sites

Radioactivity is a threat to all living things. Machines that are made of metals and composites can handle high levels of radioactivity without becoming damaged and they are widely used in the nuclear industry. In the future, there will be a growing number of nuclear sites that require dismantling and decontaminating. The role of automated machines and robots will be essential in this process, known as decommissioning.

Fire-fighting robots

Despite the safeguards that will be incorporated into future buildings, the risk of fire will always remain. Even sophisticated sprinkler systems may be ineffective against a major blaze. By 2020, the use of fire-fighting robots will be standard practice in many places. These will use a range of heat sensors and an internal map of the building to find a way into the heart of the fire area. Once there, the robots will extinguish the fire with foams and other substances.

△ *Robug 3* is a highly versatile robot that has the ability to scale walls and ceilings. It uses powerful suckers driven by compressed air to create a partial vacuum under each of its eight feet.

▽ *Dante* is an eight-legged robot designed to negotiate treacherous, unstable terrrain. It has successfully made its way into the mouth of the Alaskan volcano, Mt. Spurr.

UNDERWATER MACHINES

Over 70 per cent of our planet is covered by water. Our seas and oceans not only contain marine life but also a huge supply of valuable minerals. As land-based resources become over-stretched or exhausted, we will venture more and more underwater in search of new supplies. We will also explore the oceans to keep watch on their ecosystems. Much of this work will be performed by unmanned intelligent machines called autonomous underwater vehicles or AUVs.

△ Early diving apparatus, such as the Klingart diving suit from the later 1700s, only worked at shallow depths.

△ A modern deep-sea diving apparatus encloses the diver in an ultra-tough shell, resistant to depths of up to 600m.

Machine advantages

One of the major problems faced by people exploring underwater is that, the deeper you go, the greater the water pressure – the pressure doubles every ten metres you descend. It is far easier to construct unmanned machines that are capable of withstanding the immense pressures found at great depths. Unmanned machines are cheaper to build than manned submersibles, more manoeuvrable and involve no risk to human life.

Independence

At present, remote operated vehicles (ROVs) are controlled by a human operator on the surface and linked by a long cable called a tether. In the future, however, AUVs are likely to take over their role. Using complex sensor and control systems, these machines will operate without direct human control. By 2010, AUVs will be mapping the seabed as well as maintaining underwater cables and pipelines.

◁ Small underwater settlements, holding up to 30 people, may be with us by 2025. Samples of minerals, rocks and living things will be collected by small, multi-armed machines. Core drillers will take samples from layers of rock.

△▷ *Jason Jr* is a ROV controlled by operators aboard the manned submersible *Alvin*. *Jason Jr* successfully investigated and photographed the wreck of the *Titanic*.

Mineral resources

It has been estimated that there are over 200 billion tonnes of minerals, including metals, in the planet's seas and oceans. Manganese nodules, for example, litter many parts of the ocean floor. So far, it has not been practical to extract these types of materials from seawater. However, mining the oceans using AUVs and other machines is likely to prove far more effective.

Man vs Machines?

Manned spacecraft allow first-hand human experience of space to be charted, such as the effects of zero gravity on the human body and mind. However, there is no air, water or food in space. It all has to be carried along with living quarters for the astronauts. Spacecraft that can support life are far more expensive and complex to build than unmanned probes so a mixture of manned and unmanned missions is likely to continue long into the future.

△ The successor to the *Space Shuttle* will be based on the *X-33* and is scheduled for launch in 2005.

MACHINES IN SPACE 1

Rockets developed as weapons by the Germans during World War 11 helped to launch the space age. At first, unmanned space probes, launched by rockets, orbited the planet. Astronauts soon followed. These human pioneers relied on the most advanced machinery and technology of their time to keep them alive and get them safely home. Machines paved the way for further manned exploration, first to the Moon, in preparation for the manned landings between 1969 and 1972, and then out into the Solar System. A number of probes are currently travelling to the far reaches of the Solar System and beyond.

△ The *Atlas-Mercury* rocket launched the US's first manned spaceflight, in 1962. Astronaut John Glenn orbited the Earth three times before returning to the Earth.

One-way ticket

Many unmanned machines have been sent into space with zero expectation of their recovery. Probes have been sent near the Sun or onto hostile planet surfaces such as Mercury and Venus. Others have journeyed right through the Solar System and out into deep space. Experiments and sensors on board the probes are designed to run automatically, sending back data via high-frequency radio waves.

△ In November 2004, the *Huygens* probe will be dropped from the *Cassini* orbiter into the atmosphere of Titan, Saturn's largest moon.

◁ Launched in 1977, *Voyager 1* is now the most distant space probe, 10.5 billion km away from the Earth. Radio signals sent by *Voyager* take almost 10 hours to reach the Earth.

◁ The *Apollo 11* mission in 1969, was the first to land men on the Moon. A range of experiments was also deployed.

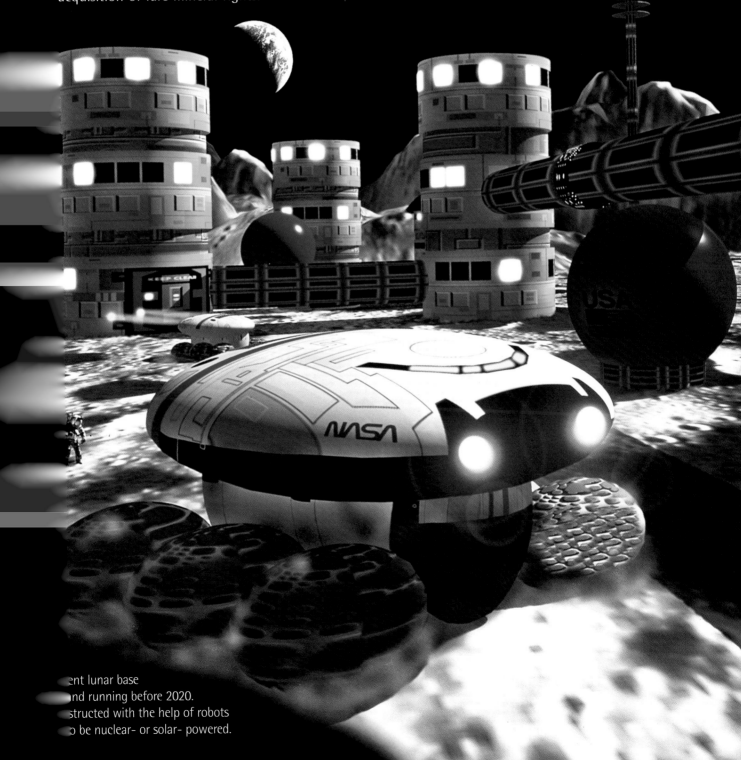

...on revisited

...interest in the Moon and the establishment ...manent research colony may be awakened ...onwards. The scientific motivation is likely ...from important breakthroughs from the ...nal *Space Station* (ISS), the establishment of ...oservatory on the far side of the Moon and ...ry work on manned missions to Mars. ...nercial backing would probably come from ...ti-national companies interested in the ...acquisition of rare mineral rights.

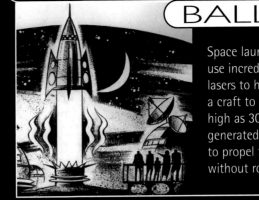

Space launches by 2100 may use incredibly high-powered lasers to heat the air below a craft to temperatures as high as 30,000°C. The thrust generated could be enough to propel the craft into orbit without rockets.

...ent lunar base
...nd running before 2020.
...structed with the help of robots
...o be nuclear- or solar- powered.

MACHINES IN SPACE 2

Huge amounts of money, time and effort are required to send machines and people into space. The *International Space Station* (*ISS*), launched in 1998, marks a new age of joint international effort that is likely to kickstart a boom in space technology. Lessons learned from its design, construction and operation will provide the basis for bigger and better space stations. The *ISS* and future stations will greatly increase our understanding of space science – especially the effects of microgravity, or weightlessness. This is likely to lead to the development of new materials and industrial processes.

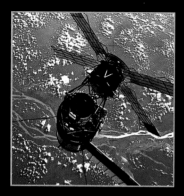

△ *Skylab*, launched in 1973, was America's first space station. It proved that humans could live and work in space for extended periods.

△ Control of the Russian *Mir* space station, launched in 1986, is highly automated. Only 13% of its operations require human intervention.

Stepping stone

The *ISS* is a joint project between 15 different countries including the United States, Canada, Russia, Japan and Britain. At least 45 missions will be involved in constructing the most ambitious man-made structure ever built in space. Powered by huge arrays of solar cells and equipped with six laboratories, the *ISS* will provide more than a decade of active service after it is completed in 2004.

△ Working in space involves a combination of machines and astronauts equipped for extra-vehicular activity (EVA). Here, a satellite capturing device is fitted to the end of a space shuttle's robot arm.

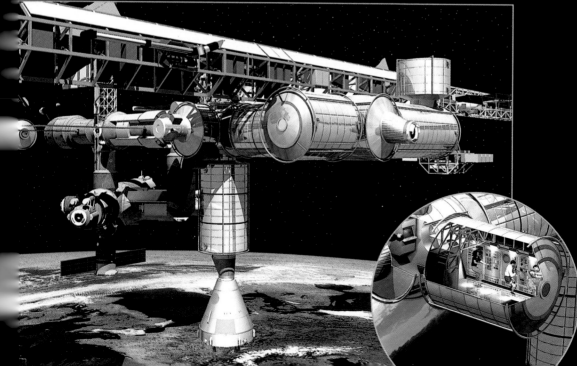

◁▽ One of the *International Space Station*'s many features will be the Columbus Orbital Facility. This pressurized module will be used to study the effects of microgravity on materials and living matter.

▷ Rotating space hotels, shaped like a bicycle wheel, may orbit Earth by 2040. The spinning motion will create artificial gravity in the outer wheel of the hotel.

All hands on deck

Building any structure in space creates unique demands. Components must be ferried into space aboard shuttles and modules launched by rockets. Once in space, astronauts and robots need to work together. Tele-operated robot cameras travel around the site providing all-round views while dextrous robot grippers manipulate parts into place. Future constructions will be assembled by robots

Alternative destination

The space programme of the 1960s and 1970s generated many unexpected advances in mechanics, robotics, medicine and computer development. Experiments that take place on future space stations are likely to lead to new areas of scientific research. Space stations could also be used as factories to manufacture new materials or, one day, even as holiday destinations for space tourists.

OUR NEW HOME

Much of the human race's drive into space has been to learn about the planets and moons that are the Earth's neighbours. From the *Apollo* Moon landings to probes such as *Voyager* and *Mariner*, sent on fly-past missions near the major planets, machines have been central to the exploration of other worlds. The planetary rovers and probes of the 1990s were mostly controlled by high frequency radio wave signals sent from mission control on the Earth. Machines sent out to other planets after 2010 will be highly intelligent and able to act independently using information gathered by an array of sensors. The information that machines send back to the Earth will pave the way for manned missions to Mars from 2025 onwards with the hope that, one day, we will be able to colonize the planet.

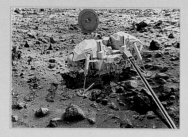

△ *Viking I* was the very first manufactured object to land on the surface of another planet. It reached Mars in 1975 and took soil samples and pictures which were relayed back to mission control on the Earth.

△In 1997, the *Sojourner* robot, carried by the *Pathfinder* probe, landed on Mars. *Sojourner* was instructed by radio signals sent from the Earth, but it also used its own sensors to plot a route to a specified target area.

Biospheres

Closed-ecology units, sometimes known as biospheres, may be sent to Mars first. These would be constructed by autonomous machines and robots before astronauts arrive to live inside them. The units would be closed off from the Martian environment, only taking in solar energy from outside. All wastes would be recycled and oxygen would be generated using plants inside the unit.

A suitable planet

Terraforming is the most ambitious of all future plans for settling on other planets. Terraforming means changing the entire environment of a planet and its atmosphere so that humans, plants and animals can live there. Mars, with its low atmospheric pressure and polar ice caps, is the most promising planet for terraforming.

Temperature rising

Mars needs to be warmed up and a thicker atmosphere created if the planet is to be terraformed. To achieve this, gases could be pumped into the Martian atmosphere to create a greenhouse effect that would trap more of the Sun's heat. If frost and part of the polar ice caps can be melted, they will provide both water on the ground and water vapour in the atmosphere. Genetically engineered bacteria and microbes that absorb carbon dioxide and give out oxygen could be introduced.

Although terraforming is a process that would take many thousands of years, we should not underestimate what the future will bring.

△ Closed-ecology units, such as the two-acre *Biosphere 2* in Arizona, US, have already been successfully built on the Earth.

△ Thousands of years from now terraforming might transform Mars, creating water reserves and a breathable atmosphere. Lightweight structures could take advantage of the low gravity, while unmanned machines could ferry materials and perform maintenance work.

GLOSSARY

Alternative energies Any source of energy that does not rely on the burning of fossil fuels (gas, coal and oil) or nuclear power. Alternative energies include geothermal power, solar power and hydroelectric power.

Artificial Intelligence (AI) The ability of machines to do intelligent things such as making decisions based on given information.

Autonomous Used to describe a machine, usually a robot, that does not depend on a human controller to perform all of its functions.

Biometrics The measurement of a person's features from finger- and handprints to eye characteristics.

Composite materials Artificial materials that feature a mixture of different materials woven or bonded together.

Geothermal power Power generated by using heat from inside the Earth.

Gravity The force of attraction between two bodies.

Laser A highly focused beam of light or other radiation used to cut through objects or to carry information through optical fibres.

Microchip A small but complex electronic device in which millions of transistors and other components are mounted on a single slice of material, usually silicon, to form an 'integrated circuit'.

Microprocessor A type of microchip that can be programmed to perform calculations or control machinery. Microprocessors are the thinking components of many machines including robots and computers.

Nanotechnology Technology created to and working at a nanometric scale. A nanometre is equal to one billionth of a metre.

Nuclear fission Splitting the nucleus of atoms or molecules to generate enormous amounts of power.

Nuclear fusion Forcing atoms to collide and fuse together which potentially generates vast amounts of power. Fusion is the process that takes place in the Sun's core.

Pneumatics A drive system that uses a gas such as air to provide power.

Radioactivity The release of electro-magnetic energy called radiation from the nuclei of unstable atoms.

Recycling Putting waste substances back into some form of productive use, such as the creation of newspaper out of recycled waste paper.

Renewable resources Materials and energies that can be used without risk of them running out. Examples of renewable resources include solar power, wave power and crops.

Sensor A device that provides a computer or microprocessor with external information about its surroundings such as temperature, sound, movement or light.

SMA Short for shape memory alloy. This is a new material capable of remembering its original shape and returning to it after being manipulated.

Smart card A card with a built-in microprocessor that contains personal information and can be used for activities such as shopping and banking.

Smart machine A machine or system that uses sensors and a microprocessor to make it behave in an intelligent way, for example, by remembering or predicting a user's actions.

Stealth A collection of technologies that work together to make a vehicle (usually an aircraft) less observable to radar and other forms of sensing.

Streamlining The shaping of a machine so that it travels through gases or liquids more smoothly and efficiently.

Superconductivity The ability of certain materials at very low temperatures to conduct electricity with little resistance.

Telecommunications The transmission and reception of information-carrying signals over a distance. Examples of telecommunications include the telephone, radio and television.

Tele-operation A system that allows a human to control or operate a machine from a distance.

Terraforming The modification of the entire environment of a planet and its atmosphere to enable Earth-styled flora and fauna to live there.

Transistor A small electronic switch that replaced the cumbersome and less reliable vacuum tubes in electric circuitry and helped make possible small, powerful microchips.

Ultrasound A sensing system that uses very high frequency sounds that are outside the range of human hearing.

Virtual reality A system that uses computers to generate an artificial environment with which a human user can interact.

WEBSITES

There are many websites related to machines and technology and how these will develop in the future.

If you are interested in learning more about nanotechnology and micro-machinery, a great starting-point can be found at:
http://www.lucifer.com/~sean/n-mnt.html

For an up-to-the-minute account of *Space Shuttle* missions and how the construction of the *International Space Station* is progressing, visit NASA's official Space Station website at:
http://spaceflight.nasa.gov/station/index.html

Running since 1996, the Cool Robot Of The Week website sends you to the web pages of many of the leading robotics laboratories around the world. It can be found at:
http://ranier.hq.nasa.gov/telerobotics_page/coolrobots.html

MIT Labs have been at the forefront of machine and technology advances for decades. They publish an exciting and absorbing magazine called *Technology Review*. The online version can be accessed at:
http://www.techreview.com/currnt.htm

To find out more about any area of robots, robotics and automated machinery, look to the frequently asked questions section of Carnegie-Mellon University's robotics pages at:
http://www.frc.ri.cmu.edu/robotics-faq/

A fascinating look at how the terraforming of another planet such as Mars may be achieved can be found at:
http://www.concentric.net/~stysk/uststuff/terraform.htm

To keep up with news of the latest developments in technology and their future, try the site of the US magazine *Popular Science* at:
http://www.popsci.com/

Finally, for an interesting and thought-provoking collection of insights into what the future might bring for power, machinery and the way we live in the middle of the 21st century, head over to *21st Century Creative Alternatives*. The website can be found at:
http://web0.tiac.net/users/seeker/IT21stlinks.html

PLACES OF INTEREST

Many museums and science centres around the world have displays and exhibitions that highlight some of the latest and forthcoming developments in machines and technology.

The Science Museum (London) A major expansion, opening in the year 2000, includes a state-of-the-art introduction to the digital revolution and an exhibition called *Future Space* where visitors are encouraged to explore how science and technology may affect their lives in the future.

The Imperial War Museum (London) carries exhibits devoted to warfare and military intelligence. Its new extension, to be built in Manchester (opening 2001) will tell the story of conflict during the 20th century.

The Museum of Science and Industry (Manchester) in the centre of the city has a number of extensive exhibitions on the many forms of power of the past and future, as well as transport and space machines.

The National Air and Space Museum (Washington D.C.) is part of the Smithsonian group of museums. It has many galleries devoted to both the history of space flight and exploration as well as exhibits and displays on what the future might bring.

The California Science Center (Exposition Park, Los Angeles) features the *Creative World* which examines how humans have built structures and machines to enhance their environment.

Further reading:

Visions by Michio Kaku
(Oxford University Press/1998)
A fascinating book by an American professor, *Visions* takes you on a journey through the key technologies that will alter our lives in the 21st century.

The Next 500 Years by Adrian Berry
(Hodder Headline/1996)
A bold book based on looking centuries ahead and predicting the possibilities of colonization of the Moon and Mars, human travel outside our Solar System and many great changes to life on the Earth.

INDEX

ACKNOWLEDGEMENTS

The publishers would like to thank the following illustrators for
their contribution to this book:

Arcana 40-41; Julian Baum 14-15, 16-17, 27 c, 52-53, 54 br
58-59; Graham Humphries 19 tr, 23 tr, 44 br, 55tr; Alex Pang
10-11, 22-23, 24-25, 28-29, 38-39, 46-47, 56-57; Mark
Preston 6-7, 8-9, 12-13, 19 c, 20-21, 32-33, 42-43 48-49.

The publishers would like to thank the following
for supplying photographs:

Cover (front) cl Science Photo Library/600 Group Fanuc/David
Parker tl Science Photo Library/Sam Ogden; Cover (back) br
Science Photo Library/Brian Brake; 6 c Science Photo
Library/Sam Ogden, br Science Photo Library/Brian Brake; 8 tl
Science Photo Library/600 Group Fanuc/David Parker, tr Sylvia
Corday Photo Library Ltd, cl Mary Evans Picture Library, c
Science & Society Picture Library/Science Museum, cr Hulton
Getty (car), cr Science & Society Picture Library; 9 tl Xerox
PARC/Dr K.Eric Drexler and Dr Ralph Merkle, tr Science Photo
Library/Sam Ogden, cl Science Photo Library/Brian Brake; 10 tl
The Bridgeman Art Library/Private Collection, bl Hulton Getty;
11 tr Science Photo Library/Brian Brake, c J.S.Automation, br
Science Photo Library/Sam Ogden; 12 bl The Bridgeman Art
Library/Private Collection; 13 t Science Photo Library/Peter
Menzel, b The Ronald Grant Archive; 14 tl Science & Society
Picture Library, tr Science Photo Library/Tony Craddock; 15 tl
Institut fuer Mikrotechnik,Mainz GmbH, Germany, tr Science
Photo Library/Manfred Kage; 16 tl Moorfields Eye Hospital, bl
IBM, br Xerox PARC/DR K.Eric Drexler and Dr Ralph Merkle; 18
tl Science Photo Library/Ken Eward, tr Science Photo Library/Ken
Eward, cl Mary Evans Picture Library, br Tony Stone
Images/Dennis O'Clair; 19 tl Science Photo Library/Eye of
Science, bc Science Photo Library/Peter Menzel, br Science Photo
Library/Ken Eward; 20 c Science Photo Library/Martin Bond, bl
Science & Society Picture Library/Science Museum, br Mary
Evans Picture Library; 22 cr Environmental Images/Martin Bond,
tl Still Pictures, cl Hutchinson Library; 23 tl Science Photo
Library/D.A.Peel; 24 tl Hulton Getty; 25 tl JET Joint
Undertaking, cr Frank Spooner Pictures/Gamma-Liaison, bl
Science Photo Library/Martin Bond, br Mary Evans Picture
Library; 26 tl Camera Press/Ralph Crane, cl Science Photo
Library/Martin Bond, cr Science Photo Library/Alex Bartel, br
Honda (UK); 26-27 b Science Photo Library/Tommaso
Guicciardini; 27 t Geoscience Features Picture Library; 28 tl The
Bridgeman Art Library/Fitzwilliam Museum, University of
Cambridge, cl Rex Features, bl Science Photo Library/David
Parker; 29 tl Science Photo Library/Martin Bond; 30 tl Science &
Society Picture Library/Science Museum/Clive Streeter, bl Frank
Spooner Pictures/Gamma-Liaison; 30-31 c Science Photo
Library/NASA, 31 t Mary Evans Picture Library, cr Science &
Society Picture Library/National Railway Museum, bc Science &
Society Picture Library/Bousfield/BKK, br Science Photo
Library/Chemical Design Ltd, 32 c Science Photo Library/Beinat,
Jerrican, cr TRH/NASM, r Science Photo Library/US Navy, bl
Hulton Getty, (revolver) ET Archive, bc Science Photo Library,
32-33 b Science Photo Library/Beinat, Jerrican, 33 cl The

Aviation Picture Library/Austin J. Brown, c TRH/NASM, br /B.
Kraft; 34 tl Camera Press/Vario-Press, cl Rex Features/Peter
Brooker, cr Corbis UK/Everett, bl Science Photo Library/David
Ducros; 35 t The Aviation Picture Library/Austin J. Brown, cl
CCS Communication Control System Ltd, bl Tony Stone
Images/Chad Slattery, bc Tony Stone Images/Dennis O'Clair, br
Tony Stone Images/Dennis O'Clair; 36 t TRH, cl Science &
Society Picture Library, cr TRH/Armourshield Ltd, bl Frank
Spooner Pictures; 36-37 br Frank Spooner Pictures/J.M. Turpin;
37 t Photo Press, The Defence Picture Library, cl Rex
Features/Dennis Cameron, tc (bullet) Jaycor, bc Rex
Features/Dennis Cameron, bl SPAWAR, br Science & Society
Picture Library; 38 tl Northrop Grumman Corporation, cl Hulton
Getty; 39 tc Frank Spooner Pictures /Gamma, tr Frank Spooner
Pictures/Gamma; 40 tl TRH/Imperial War Museum; 41 tl The
Aviation Picture Library/Matra Systemes & Information, tr Frank
Spooner Pictures/Gamma, cl TRH/ Thomson-CSF, 43 cl Frank
Spooner Pictures/Charles/Liaison, (Satellite) Camera Press; cl
NASA, cr Diners Club International, (Sputnik) Science Photo
Library/Novosti, 44 c Frank Spooner Pictures/Liaison, bl
Philips/Visions of the Future; 45 cr Softroom/Design: J.Jones/
T.Spencer, b /Design: J.Jones/ T.Spencer, 46 tl Frank Spooner
Pictures/Gamma-Liaison, cl Science Photo Library/Hank Morgan,
47 tc Mary Evans Picture Library, cr Science Photo Library/Hank
Morgan, br Science Photo Library/Peter Yates; 48 tc Hulton
Getty; c Frank Spooner Pictures/Gamma-Liaison; 49 tr Frank
Spooner Pictures/Gamma-Liaison, c Science Photo Library/
Jerrican Daudier; 50 tl Science Photo Library/Spencer Grant, cl
Science Photo Library/Hank Morgan, b BNFL; 51 t Frank
Spooner Pictures/FSP/Gamma/Tom Kidd, b NASA Ames Research
Center; 52 tl Mary Evans Picture Library; 53 tr Frank Spooner
Pictures/Gamma-Liaison, cr Frank Spooner Pictures/Gamma-
Liaison; 54 tr Lockheed Martin, cl Science Photo Library/NASA,
b NASA; 55 b Science Photo Library/Victor Habbick Visions; 56
tl Science Photo Library/NASA, cl Science Photo Library/NASA, cr
Science Photo Library/NASA, bl Science Photo Library/David
Ducros, bc Science Photo Library/David Ducros; 58 tl Science
Photo Library; 59 tc Science Photo Library/Peter Menzel.

Key: b = bottom, c = centre, l =left, r = right, t = top.

Every effort has been made to trace the copyright holders
of the photographs. The publishers apologize for any
inconvenience caused.

The publishers would also like to thank the following:
Martin Cross, Keith Goodall of Stantec, Robert Kemp,
Gerhart Meurer of John Hopkins University, Dr. Andrew
Rudge of BNFL and Michael White.